Francis Frith's
AROUND CHESTER

Francis Frith's
AROUND CHESTER

◆

Clive Hardy

FRITH
BOOK Co

First published in the United Kingdom in 1999 by
Frith Book Company Ltd

Hardback Edition
ISBN 1-85937-090-X

Paperback Edition 2001
ISBN 1-85937-382-8

British Library Cataloguing in Publication Data

Francis Frith's Around Chester
Clive Hardy

Frith Book Company Ltd
Frith's Barn, Teffont,
Salisbury, Wiltshire SP3 5QP
Tel: +44 (0) 1722 716 376
Email: info@francisfrith.co.uk
www.francisfrith.co.uk

Printed and bound in Great Britain

AS WITH ANY HISTORICAL DATABASE THE FRITH ARCHIVE IS CONSTANTLY BEING CORRECTED AND IMPROVED
AND THE PUBLISHERS WOULD WELCOME INFORMATION ON OMISSIONS OR INACCURACIES

CONTENTS

FRANCIS FRITH: *Victorian Pioneer*

FRANCIS FRITH, Victorian founder of the world-famous photographic archive, was a complex and multitudinous man. A devout Quaker and a highly successful Victorian businessman, he was both philosophic by nature and pioneering in outlook.

By 1855 Francis Frith had already established a wholesale grocery business in Liverpool, and sold it for the astonishing sum of £200,000, which is the equivalent today of over £15,000,000. Now a multi-millionaire, he was able to indulge his passion for travel. As a child he had pored over travel books written by early explorers, and his fancy and imagination had been stirred by family holidays to the sublime mountain regions of Wales and Scotland. 'What a land of spirit-stirring and enriching scenes and places!' he had written. He was to return to these scenes of grandeur in later years to 'recapture the thousands of vivid and tender memories', but with a different purpose. Now in his thirties, and captivated by the new science of photography, Frith

set out on a series of pioneering journeys to the Nile regions that occupied him from 1856 until 1860.

INTRIGUE AND ADVENTURE

He took with him on his travels a specially-designed wicker carriage that acted as both dark-room and sleeping chamber. These far-flung journeys were packed with intrigue and adventure. In his life story, written when he was sixty-three, Frith tells of being held captive by bandits, and of fighting 'an awful midnight battle to the very point of surrender with a deadly pack of hungry, wild dogs'. Sporting flowing Arab costume, Frith arrived at Akaba by camel seventy years before Lawrence, where he encountered 'desert princes and rival sheikhs, blazing with jewel-hilted swords'.

During these extraordinary adventures he was assiduously exploring the desert regions bordering the Nile and patiently recording the antiquities and peoples with his camera. He was the first photographer to venture beyond the sixth cataract. Africa was still the mysterious 'Dark Continent', and Stanley and Livingstone's historic meeting was a decade into the future. The conditions for picture taking confound belief. He laboured for hours in his wicker dark-room in the sweltering heat of the desert, while the volatile chemicals fizzed dangerously in their trays. Often he was forced to work in remote tombs and caves where conditions were cooler. Back in London he exhibited his photographs and was 'rapturously cheered' by members of the Royal Society. His reputation as a photographer was made overnight. An eminent modern historian has likened their impact on the population of the time to that on our own generation of the first photographs taken on the surface of the moon.

VENTURE OF A LIFE-TIME

Characteristically, Frith quickly spotted the opportunity to create a new business as a specialist publisher of photographs. He lived in an era of immense and sometimes violent change. For the poor in the early part of Victoria's reign work was a drudge and the hours long, and people had precious little free time to enjoy themselves.

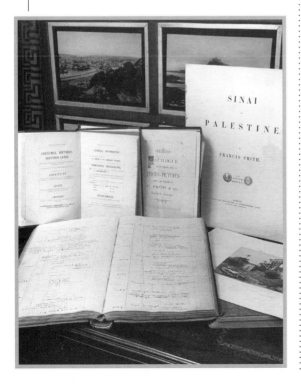

Most had no transport other than a cart or gig at their disposal, and had not travelled far beyond the boundaries of their own town or village. However, by the 1870s, the railways had threaded their way across the country, and Bank Holidays and half-day Saturdays had been made obligatory by Act of Parliament. All of a sudden the ordinary working man and his family were able to enjoy days out and see a little more of the world.

With characteristic business acumen, Francis Frith foresaw that these new tourists would enjoy having souvenirs to commemorate their days out. In 1860 he married Mary Ann Rosling and set out with the intention of photographing every city, town and village in Britain. For the next thirty years he travelled the country by train and by pony and trap, producing fine photographs of seaside resorts and beauty spots that were keenly bought by millions of Victorians. These prints were painstakingly pasted into family albums and pored over during the dark nights of winter, rekindling precious memories of summer excursions.

THE RISE OF FRITH & CO

Frith's studio was soon supplying retail shops all over the country. To meet the demand he gathered about him a small team of photographers, and published the work of independent artist-photographers of the calibre of Roger Fenton and Francis Bedford. In order to gain some understanding of the scale of Frith's business one only has to look at the catalogue issued by Frith & Co in 1886: it runs to some 670

pages, listing not only many thousands of views of the British Isles but also many photographs of most European countries, and China, Japan, the USA and Canada – note the sample page shown above from the hand-written *Frith & Co* ledgers detailing pictures taken. By 1890 Frith had created the greatest specialist photographic publishing company in the world, with over 2,000 outlets – more than the combined number that Boots and WH Smith have today! The picture on the right shows the *Frith & Co* display board at Ingleton in the Yorkshire Dales. Beautifully constructed with mahogany frame and gilt inserts, it could display up to a dozen local scenes.

POSTCARD BONANZA

The ever-popular holiday postcard we know today took many years to develop. In 1870 the Post Office issued the first plain cards, with a pre-printed stamp on one face. In 1894 they allowed other publishers' cards to be sent through the mail with an attached adhesive halfpenny stamp. Demand grew rapidly, and in 1895 a new size of postcard was permitted called the court card, but there was little room for illustration. In 1899, a year after Frith's death, a new card measuring 5.5 x 3.5 inches became the standard format, but it was not until 1902 that the divided back came into being, with address and message on one face and a full-size illustration on the other. *Frith & Co* were in the vanguard of postcard development, and Frith's sons Eustace and Cyril continued their father's monumental task, expanding the number of views offered to the public and recording more and more places in Britain, as the coasts and countryside were opened up to mass travel.

Francis Frith died in 1898 at his villa in Cannes, his great project still growing. The archive he created continued in business for another seventy years. By 1970 it contained over a third of a million pictures of 7,000 cities, towns and villages. The massive photographic record Frith has left to us stands as a living monument to a special and very remarkable man.

Frith's Archive: *A Unique Legacy*

FRANCIS FRITH'S legacy to us today is of immense significance and value, for the magnificent archive of evocative photographs he created provides a unique record of change in 7,000 cities, towns and villages throughout Britain over a century and more. Frith and his fellow studio photographers revisited locations many times down the years to update their views, compiling for us an enthralling and colourful pageant of British life and character.

We tend to think of Frith's sepia views of Britain as nostalgic, for most of us use them to conjure up memories of places in our own lives with which we have family associations. It often makes us forget that to Francis Frith they were records of daily life as it was actually being lived in the cities, towns and villages of his day. The Victorian age was one of great and often bewildering change for ordinary people, and though the pictures evoke an impression of slower times, life was as busy and hectic as it is today.

We are fortunate that Frith was a photographer of the people, dedicated to recording the minutiae of everyday life. For it is this sheer wealth of visual data, the painstaking chronicle of changes in dress, transport, street layouts, buildings, housing, engineering and landscape that captivates us so much today. His remarkable images offer us a powerful link with the past and with the lives of our ancestors.

TODAY'S TECHNOLOGY

Computers have now made it possible for Frith's many thousands of images to be accessed almost instantly. In the Frith archive today, each photograph is carefully 'digitised' then stored on a CD Rom. Frith archivists can locate a single photograph amongst thousands within seconds. Views can be catalogued and sorted under a variety of categories of place and content to the immediate benefit of researchers. Inexpensive reference prints can be created for them at the touch of a mouse button, and a wide range of books and other printed materials assembled and published for a wider, more general readership - in the next twelve months over a hundred Frith local history titles will be published! The

See Frith at www. francisfrith.co.uk

day-to-day workings of the archive are very different from how they were in Francis Frith's time: imagine the herculean task of sorting through eleven tons of glass negatives as Frith had to do to locate a particular sequence of pictures! Yet the archive still prides itself on maintaining the same high standards of excellence laid down by Francis Frith, including the painstaking cataloguing and indexing of every view.

It is curious to reflect on how the internet now allows researchers in America and elsewhere greater instant access to the archive than Frith himself ever enjoyed. Many thousands of individual views can be called up on screen within seconds on one of the Frith internet sites, enabling people living continents away to revisit the streets of their ancestral home town, or view places in Britain where they have enjoyed holidays. Many overseas researchers welcome the chance to view special theme selections, such as transport, sports, costume and ancient monuments.

We are certain that Francis Frith would have heartily approved of these modern developments, for he himself was always working at the very limits of Victorian photographic technology.

THE VALUE OF THE ARCHIVE TODAY

Because of the benefits brought by the computer, Frith's images are increasingly studied by social historians, by researchers into genealogy and ancestory, by architects, town planners, and by teachers and schoolchildren involved in local history projects. In addition, the archive offers every one of us a unique opportunity to examine the places where we and our families have lived and worked down the years. Immensely successful in Frith's own era, the archive is now, a century and more on, entering a new phase of popularity.

THE PAST IN TUNE WITH THE FUTURE

Historians consider the Francis Frith Collection to be of prime national importance. It is the only archive of its kind remaining in private ownership and has been valued at a million pounds. However, this figure is now rapidly increasing as digital technology enables more and more people around the world to enjoy its benefits.

Francis Frith's archive is now housed in an historic timber barn in the beautiful village of Teffont in Wiltshire. Its founder would not recognize the archive office as it is today. In place of the many thousands of dusty boxes containing glass plate negatives and an all-pervading odour of photographic chemicals, there are now ranks of computer screens. He would be amazed to watch his images travelling round the world at unimaginable speeds through network and internet lines.

The archive's future is both bright and exciting. Francis Frith, with his unshakeable belief in making photographs available to the greatest number of people, would undoubtedly approve of what is being done today with his lifetime's work. His photographs, depicting our shared past, are now bringing pleasure and enlightenment to millions around the world a century and more after his death.

CHESTER – *An Introduction*

FEW BRITISH CITIES have changed as little as Chester in the last one hundred years. Saved from heavy industry by the silting up of the Dee, in the 19th century it was a quiet country town providing a prosperous farming county with facilities for business, lawsuits and entertainment.

The strategic importance of the site now occupied by Chester was realised by the Romans during their campaigns against the Brigantes and the Welsh. The site was on the north bank of the Dee at the lowest bridging point before the estuary. The fortress covered 56 acres and comprised an outer ditch and a turfed rampart topped by a wooden palisade, together with wooden gatehouses and towers. Capable of holding a legion, the huge fortress was completed in AD79-80, but at some time around AD100 reconstruction work began to make Deva, as it was called, a more permanent establishment. Rome was here to stay, and occupied the site for over three hundred years.

Writing in the 8th century, the Venerable Bede accorded Chester the status of a civitas, implying that it was still an important centre; we do know that a synod was held here around AD607. It was considered important enough by Aethelfrith of Northumbria for him to launch an all-out assault and destroy the place during his conquest of the area in about AD616.

In more recent times Chester was the first stop on the highly uncomfortable stagecoach route from Liverpool to London, used by those going to and from Ireland, which accounts for the city's large number of inns. Much of what we find most attractive about the Chester street scene today was built in the later decades of the 19th century. A few carefully-preserved houses of Tudor origin can still be seen, but most of the larger black-and-white buildings in Chester's main streets are such excellent imitations of the style that their lack of antiquity does not detract in any way from the pleasure they give to the visitor. Of special delight are the covered walkways at first floor level, known as The Rows. Great care was taken during the Victorian reconstruction of the city centre to retain them; they continue to provide not only an additional layer of weatherproof shopping, but a wonderful vantage point from which to view the scene below.

In these photographs there is much to please the eye; also, for those who have the opportunity to compare them with the Chester of today, there are hours of entertainment spotting the changes which have taken place. Look carefully at the people going about their daily lives at a more leisurely pace and note how quickly fashions changed at the turn of the century, both in clothes and methods of transport.

THE CITY WALLS AND KING CHARLES I TOWER 1888 20619
Built of red sandstone, the city walls form a circuit of two miles around the old city. The north and east walls follow the line of those of the Roman fortress; those on the west and south were moved so that more land could be incorporated within the city's defences. Also known as the Phoenix Tower, it was from here on 24 September 1645 that King Charles watched the Battle of Rowton Heath which took place just outside the city walls.

THE WATER TOWER 1891 28886
This tower was built in 1322 as an outwork to the tower on the north-west corner of the wall. The tower derives its name from the time when Chester was a thriving port and ships used to moor alongside it.

THE WATER TOWER 1888 20616
The remains of a Roman hypercaust, the heating system for a Roman bath, were discovered in Bridge Street in 1863 and subsequently relocated to the gardens by the Water Tower.

PARK STREET 1888 20609

These days trees screen the wall from
these alms houses in Park Street. The
large half-timbered building carries
the legend 'The fear of the Lord is a
fountain of life.'

FOREGATE
Looking toward the Eastgate 1903 49887

The Eastgate, which was the entry point of the Roman road, the Via Devana, was rebuilt as an elegant arch in 1769. When the Northgate was rebuilt in 1808 the foundations of the Roman gate were discovered. The clock standing on the top of the Eastgate was presented to the city by Edward Evans-Lloyd in 1897 to commemorate Queen Victoria's diamond jubilee. The clock was made by J B Joyce of Whitchurch, and sits on top of ornate ironwork designed by John Douglas.

FOREGATE STREET 1929 82748

Compare this picture with No 49887. The Chester Northgate Brewery Co's premises have been demolished and replaced by a half-timbered revival building housing the booksellers W H Smith. Other new arrivals are Burtons the tailors and Stewarts Ltd.

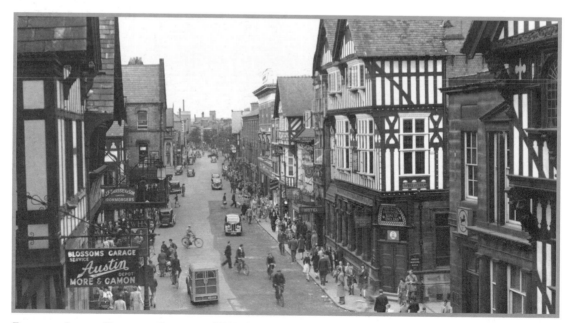

FOREGATE STREET, FROM THE EASTGATE c1955 C82065

Foregate Street was one of the city locations painted by artist Louise Rayner (1832-1924) in a work entitled 'A Busy Street'. It certainly looks busy enough in this picture. At this date J F Brassey & Son, ironmongers, are still occupying the same premises they were in at the beginning of the 20th century, though they were probably no longer horseshoe manufacturers.

FOREGATE STREET, FROM THE EASTGATE c1955 C82078
Cyclists pedal along in comparative safety, and a lady is happy to stand in the middle of the road and ask a policeman for directions. In 1955 for the first time ever the annual home sales for new cars passed the 500,000 mark, thanks in part to a reduction in income tax of 6d in the pound.

EASTGATE STREET 1891 28874

Before the development of the Tudor-style half-timbered buildings on the north side of the street, the view from the top of the Eastgate looking towards the Cross was much less impressive.

EASTGATE STREET 1895 36447

In the four years since the previous picture was taken some redevelopment of the north side of the street has taken place, though there was more to come. On the left is the 86-bedroom Grosvenor Hotel, the most expensive to stay in, though prices at the 100-bedroom Queens Hotel were not too far behind.

EASTGATE STREET 1923 73865
This view looks towards The Cross. By 1923 the number of cars in Chester was increasing; no doubt there were already complaints about the volume of traffic. By this date all the major hotels, apart from Blossoms, offered garage facilities for guests' automobiles.

EASTGATE STREET 1900 46215
By this time Eastgate was already a very sophisticated shopping area. Bollands, the confectionery shop on the right, had a high reputation and had been confectioners to the late Queen; the handcart outside bears the legend 'Wedding Cakes as supplied to the King'.

EASTGATE STREET 1888 20594

EASTGATE STREET 1929 82746

EASTGATE STREET 1888
Twelve years before the turn of the century the Eastgate looks austere without its decorative clock. But this picture does give us an uncluttered view of the Grosvenor Hotel, while on the right, Brown, Holmes & Co, silk mercers to both Her Majesty and HRH The Princess of Wales, sport the royal arms above their entrance.

◆

EASTGATE STREET 1929
Cloche hats and knee-length skirts place this picture firmly in the roaring twenties. A boy and girl on a bicycle not made for two make an arresting combination, though they are more likely to receive a lecture from the man in blue. And no matter how quickly they get home, news of their being ticked off by a bobby will somehow have got there before them.

EASTGATE STREET c1929 C82013

A tram en route to Chester General station enters a passing loop; Eastgate Street was too narrow for double track to be laid. The large half-timbered building on the left with its awnings out was built in the mid-1890s, and became the local branch of F W Woolworths. The classical building on the left dates from 1860 and was where the Westminster Bank had its Chester branch.

EASTGATE STREET 1891 28878

The Rows are a unique feature to Chester; they provide shops on two levels, the roofs of the shops at street level forming a pedestrian walkway for the shops on the second level. They are known to have existed in the 13th century. Opinion is divided as to their origins.

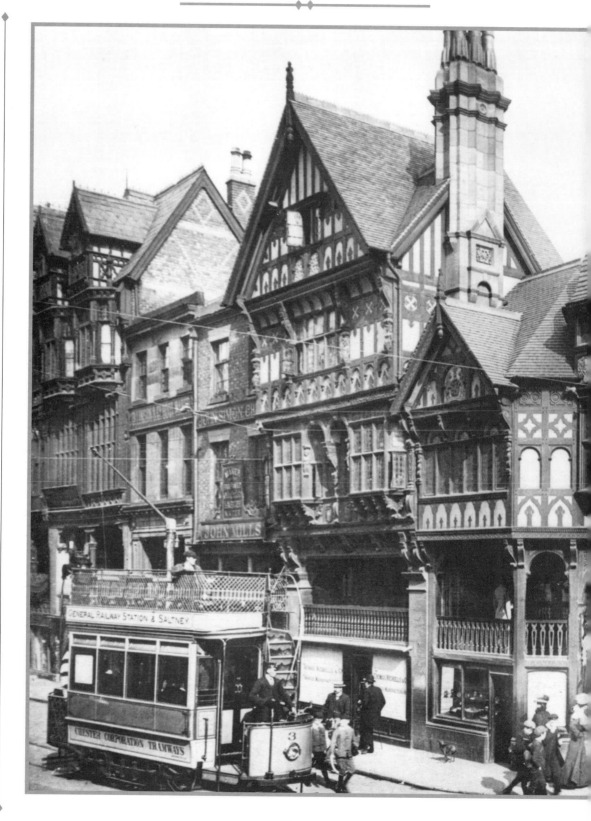

THE CROSS 1903 49881
This area of the city is known as The Cross. In Roman
times several roads met at this spot and until it was
demolished during the Civil War, a medieval cross stood
nearby. The cross was restored to its original site in 1975.

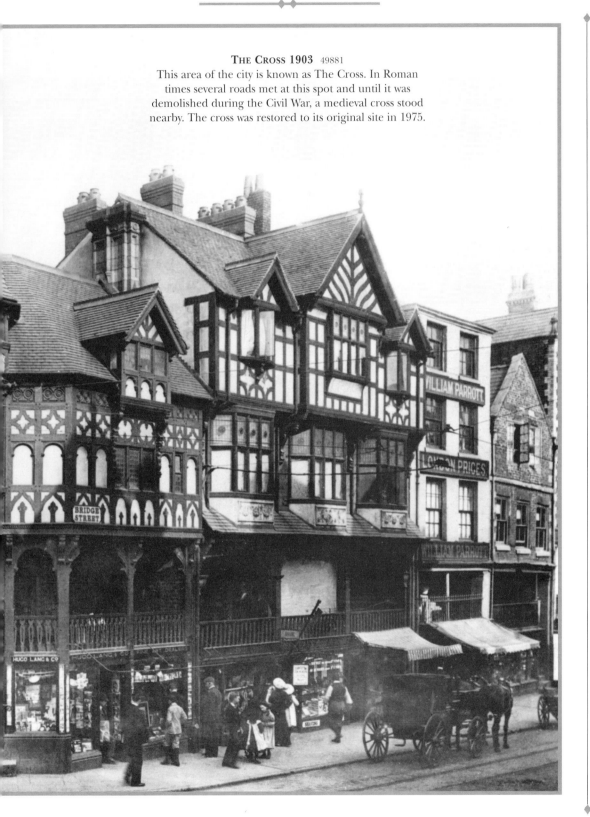

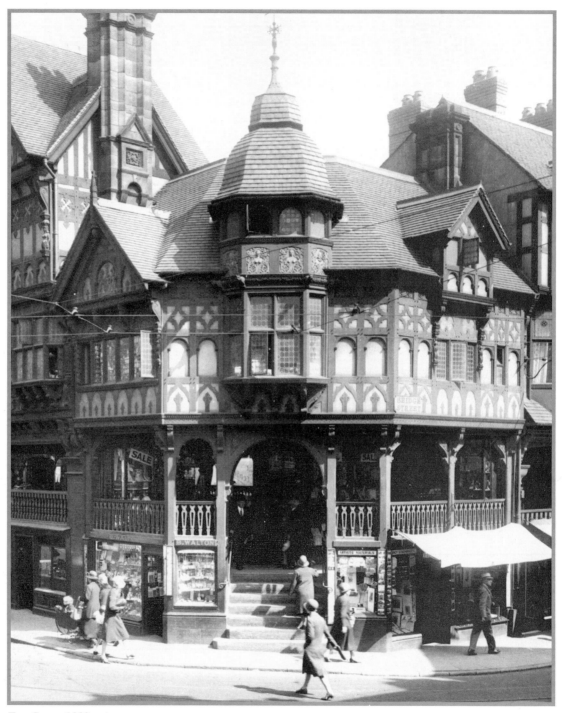

THE CROSS 1929 82744

It is sale time in Chester, with perhaps the chance to pick up the odd bargain or two. Prices in general were falling back to their pre-Great War levels, having risen dramatically during the conflict. For example, a pound of streaky bacon cost 1s 3d in 1914 and 2s 7d in 1920, but by 1933 had fallen back to 1s 5d. Similarly, butter was 1s 3d in 1914, 2s 11d in 1920 and 1s 2d in 1933.

WATERGATE STREET c1955 C82067

Of Chester's main streets, Watergate Street is the least changed and retains a natural charm. It is a continuation of Eastgate Street, and contains three of the finest half-timbered houses in England. There are Rows on both sides of Watergate Street. Above Nobletts Chocolates we have the Victoria Commercial Hotel (established 1269) which, given its great age, was conspicuous by its absence from late 19th and early 20th-century guide books for overseas visitors.

WATERGATE ROW 1863

This is one of the oldest pictures in the archive and almost certainly taken by Francis Frith himself. Of the various theories regarding the origins of the Rows, one is that they might well be an echo of a Roman pattern of domestic building; a combination of workshops, shops, the Roman equivalent of fast food outlets, and residential apartments.

◆

WATERGATE STREET 1895

In the late 19th century, the writers of tourist guides such as Baedeckers considered the Rows in Watergate Street to be the poor relations of those in other parts of the city. Certainly the building occupied by Peers looks dilapidated, as does the smaller building next to it.

WATERGATE ROW 1863 1525

WATERGATE STREET 1895 36453

WATERGATE STREET 1888 20608

Food hygiene regulations have changed somewhat since this photograph of the Leche House was taken. The house is named after the Leche family; their coat of arms can still be seen on a fireplace in one of the first floor rooms. The Rows clearly provided Maddocks the cabinetmakers with a valuable display area.

WATERGATE STREET 1888 20605
One of the most famous buildings in Chester, the God's Provident House. The house was originally built in 1652 and rebuilt in 1862. The inscription, 'God's Providence is mine inheritance', is said to commemorate the household's immunity from the plague.

STANLEY PALACE 1895 36452
In 1828 the Earl of Derby presented the city with Stanley Palace. It was built in 1591 for Peter Warburton, MP for Chester, and passed into the hands of the Stanley family through the marriage of his daughter to
Sir Thomas Stanley.

WATERGATE STREET 1888 20603
This inn on Watergate Street no longer exists. It was
probably removed in order to enlarge St Martin's
Way. Jonathan Swift once lodged in Watergate Street
at the Yacht Inn.

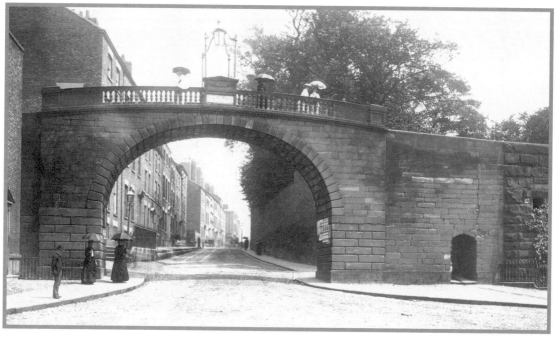

THE WATERGATE 1888 20606
Ladies protect their complexions with parasols whilst viewing Watergate Street from the parapet above the gate.
The view up the street has changed little since the gate was built in 1867.

THE NEW GRANDSTAND 1900 45420
Beyond Watergate Street is the Roodee, Chester's race course, where the Chester Cup is raced for every May. On
race days the section of the wall overlooking the track is closed to stop punters getting their racing for free.

CURZON PARK WEST 1906

The residential suburb of Curzon Park West lies across the Dee to the south-west of the race course. Cab fares in 1906 were 1s a mile for 1-2 persons, 1s 6d per mile for 3-5 persons, and fare and a half between midnight and 6.00am.

◆

HOUGH GREEN WEST 1906

The electric tramway ran from Chester General station through the town and crossed the Dee by way of the Grosvenor Bridge. It then continued to Eaton Park and Saltney. In 1906 it was more expensive to sit inside a Chester tram than on the exposed upper deck.

CURZON PARK WEST 1906 55285

HOUGH GREEN WEST 1906 55287

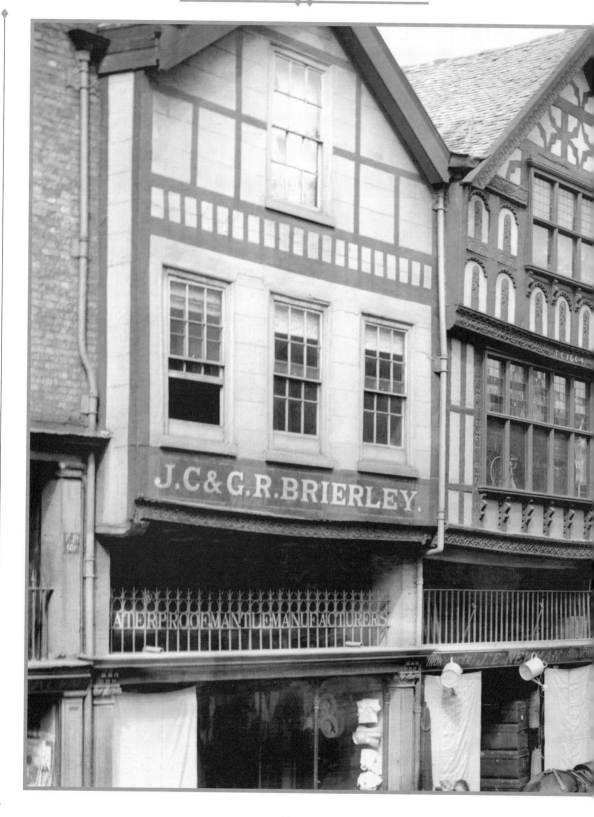

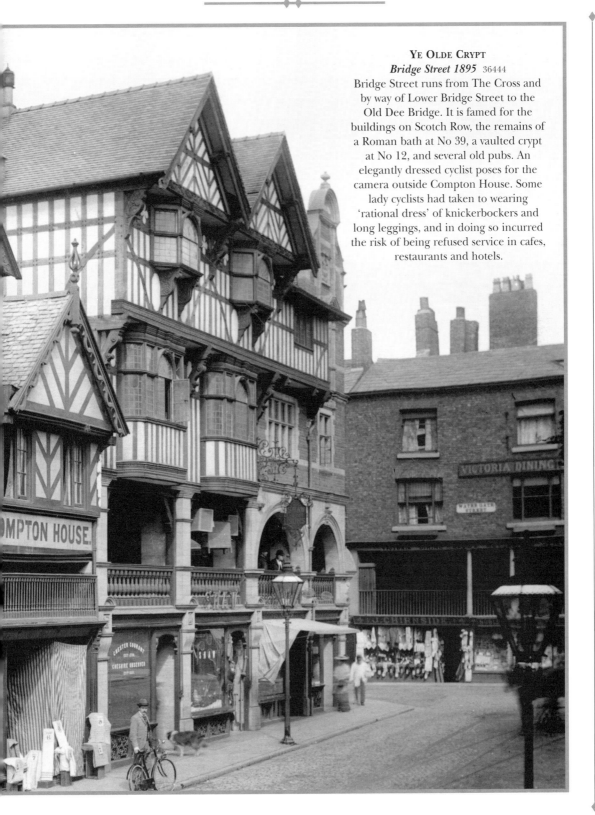

YE OLDE CRYPT
Bridge Street 1895 36444

Bridge Street runs from The Cross and by way of Lower Bridge Street to the Old Dee Bridge. It is famed for the buildings on Scotch Row, the remains of a Roman bath at No 39, a vaulted crypt at No 12, and several old pubs. An elegantly dressed cyclist poses for the camera outside Compton House. Some lady cyclists had taken to wearing 'rational dress' of knickerbockers and long leggings, and in doing so incurred the risk of being refused service in cafes, restaurants and hotels.

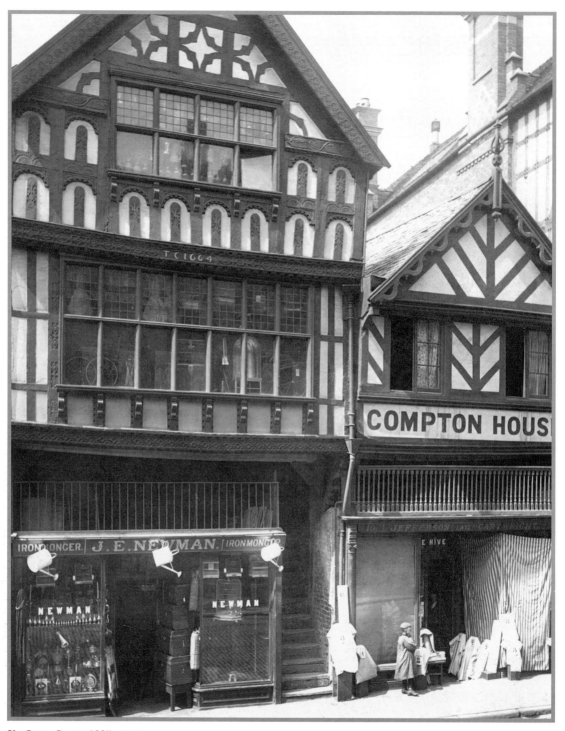

YE OLDE CRYPT 1895 36446
Here we see a close-up of Compton House and Newmans. Behind the latter is a medieval vault known as Ye Olde Crypt which dates from c1230. There are also crypts beneath No 34 Eastgate Street and Nos 11 and 13 Watergate Street.

BRIDGE STREET 1888 20595

This side of Bridge Street in the 1880s and 90s could quite easily have been renamed Ironmongers Row. As well as Newman, who had an interesting line in metal trunks and chests, bird-cages and bicycles, there was Thomas Wood & Sons for lamps and household appliances, including zinc baths, and Shaws for general goods and cutlery.

BRIDGE STREET 1903 49890

It is coming up to ten minutes to eleven by St Peter's clock as one of the new electric tramcars rattles along Bridge Street on its way to Saltney. On the left outside Hodley's is a poster announcing the postponement of the Ruabon date for Buffalo Bill's Wild West Show.

BRIDGE STREET 1903 49889

At the turn of the century, shopkeepers prided themselves on giving a personal service, and many of them employed boys with handcarts to make home deliveries. Retailers of all types - grocers, butchers, ironmongers and so on - operated mobile shops which visited outlying villages. There were also individuals who went from one village to another selling watercress, prawns, and even bolts of cloth.

BRIDGE STREET c1955 C82063

Here we see a change of pace compared to some of the previous pictures: the pavements are crowded with pedestrians and the road is heaving with traffic. 1955 was a year of newspaper and dock strikes; it was also the year in which parking meters were introduced on a trial basis in London.

BRIDGE STREET 1895 36440

The ironmonger on the right has taken every opportunity to display the variety of his wares, though the children will almost certainly be more interested in the next shop along where both Chester rock and ice cream are on sale. For those wishing to partake of something a little more wholesome, the Central Dining Rooms are just a few yards further on.

BRIDGE STREET 1891 28876
The drinking fountain with its elegant gaslamp was constructed in 1859; alas, it is no longer with us.

LOWER BRIDGE STREET 1888 20599

LOWER BRIDGE STREET 1888
The Falcon Inn at the corner of Grosvenor Street was once the town house of the Grosvenor family. This picture was taken when the building was being used as a cocoa house and billiards hall, and judging by the supporting joists it is in need of repair.

◆

LOWER BRIDGE STREET 1903
Lower Bridge Street in the days when those short of a few shillings could pay a visit to Edwin Henry Dutton, pawnbroker and jeweller, and those who did have a few shillings could go along to the bespoke tailor, where made-to-measure suits were available from as little as thirty shillings.

LOWER BRIDGE STREET 1903 49891

LOWER BRIDGE STREET 1888 20600

LOWER BRIDGE STREET 1888
The Old King's Head dates from the early 17th century, as does the Falcon Inn (1626). In 1888 landlord J Grice was offering his patrons home-brewed ale.

◆

LOWER BRIDGE STREET 1888
The King Edgar Inn on the corner of Lower Bridge Street and Shipgate Street was in need of urgent repairs. It looks as though there was once a door and a ground floor window on the Lower Bridge Street side of the building.

LOWER BRIDGE STREET 1888 20602

LOWER BRIDGE STREET 1888 20601

THE BEAR AND BILLET 1895 36449

LOWER BRIDGE STREET 1888
The Bear and Billet public house in Lower Bridge Street was built in 1664; until 1867 it was the town house of the earls of Shrewsbury. At some time during the 19th century the inn frontage was remodelled to provide the upper floors with continuous windows.

◆

THE BEAR AND BILLET 1895
By 1895 Worthingtons pale and Burton ales were brewed at Burton-upon-Trent; William Worthington had opened his brewery there in 1760 some seventeen years before William Bass. Now a part of the Bass empire, Worthington dark mild and Worthington draught bitter are brewed in Cardiff.

THE CATHEDRAL

Built of red sandstone, Chester cathedral was founded in 1092 as a Benedictine abbey on the site of an earlier Saxon church dedicated to St Werburgh. St Werburgh was a late 7th-century Saxon princess and a daughter of king Wulfhere of Mercia. Werburgh was later appointed supervisor of all the nunneries in Mercia, and died at Trentham in AD699. In AD874 St Werburgh's remains were transferred to Chester to prevent them from falling into the hands of Danish invaders.

Parts of the Norman church can still be seen, though much of the present cathedral dates from the 13th to the 16th centuries. At the Dissolution the building was saved from destruction when it was chosen as the cathedral for the newly formed diocese of Chester. A careful restoration programme was undertaken by Sir George Gilbert Scott, the well known Victorian architect, who added battlements, pinnacles and buttresses, but yearned most of all to top the tower with a tall spire.

ST WERBURGH STREET 1929 82749
St Werburgh Street runs from Eastgate Street and joins with Northgate Street near the cathedral. On this particular sunny afternoon the policeman on point duty seems to be getting respite from the traffic chaos normally associated with this part of the city.

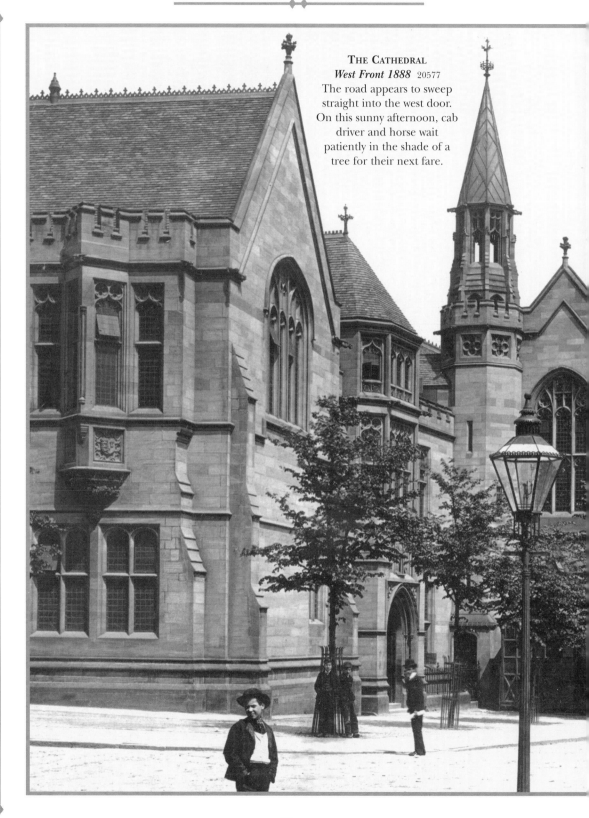

THE CATHEDRAL
West Front 1888 20577
The road appears to sweep straight into the west door. On this sunny afternoon, cab driver and horse wait patiently in the shade of a tree for their next fare.

THE CATHEDRAL, FROM THE NORTH EAST 1891 28871
Featured here is the adjoining Chapter House built in the late 13th century; it follows the classic Early English style for monastic chapter houses and vestibules by being rectangular in shape.

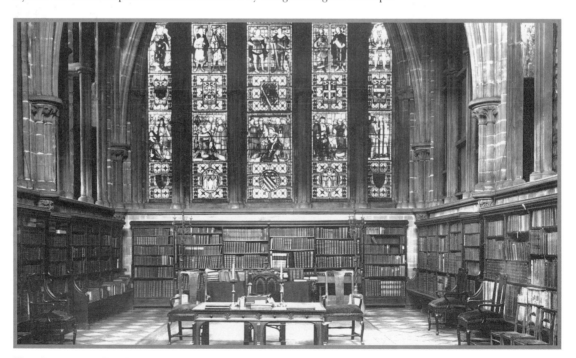

THE CATHEDRAL, THE CHAPTER HOUSE 1888 20592
This is the Chapter House in the days when it housed the cathedral library; in more recent times it has been used as a bookshop. The fine stained glass east window features scenes from the life of St Werburgh.

THE CATHEDRAL, CLOISTER GARDENS 1929 82762
This view of the garden is taken from the South Cloister. On going through the door the refectory is directly ahead, the early-Norman undercroft to our left, and the fratry and vestibule are on the right.

THE CATHEDRAL, CLOISTER GARDENS 1929 82760
At this time, the reconstruction of the cloister gardens had not long been completed. Today, instead of a fountain, an elegant statue by sculptor Stephen Broadbent graces the centre of the lily pond.

THE CATHEDRAL, CHOIR WEST 1888 20583
Intricately carved choir stalls from 1380 provide a rich and enclosed setting for choral practice. The ironwork suspended cross, by Sir George Gilbert Scott, was removed in the early years of the 20th century, possibly because it was considered to be too 'high church'; it is now in the parish church of Dunham-on-the-Hill.

THE CATHEDRAL, THE DEAN'S SEAT 1913 66108A
The Dean's seat is just one of the many superb examples of wood-carving in the stalls. Bench ends, misericords and canopies are individually carved.

THE CATHEDRAL 1913
As well as these fine examples of wood-carving, the cathedral also boasts two modern carved corbels on the exterior of the South Transept. One features Gladstone, the other Dr Kenealy.

◆

THE CATHEDRAL 1913
There are only two other places in England where the quality of the wood-carving is comparable to Chester. One is Lincoln Cathedral, the other is Beverley Minster.

THE CATHEDRAL 1913 66103

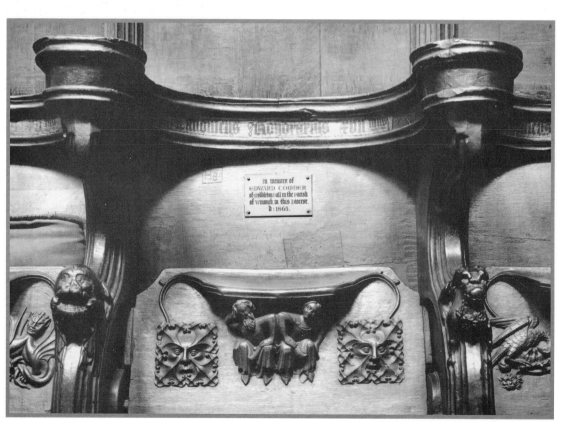

THE CATHEDRAL 1913 66105

THE CATHEDRAL, THE CRYPT 1888 20591
The undercroft on the west side of the cloister garden comprises the two vaulted aisles that once formed the abbot's cellars; above this was the guest-house. In more recent times the undercroft has been converted into a bookshop and exhibition centre.

NORTHGATE STREET 1903 49882
Northgate Street runs north from
The Cross; it is here, in the
basement of No 23, that remains
thought to belong to the
headquarters building of the XXth
Legion can be seen.

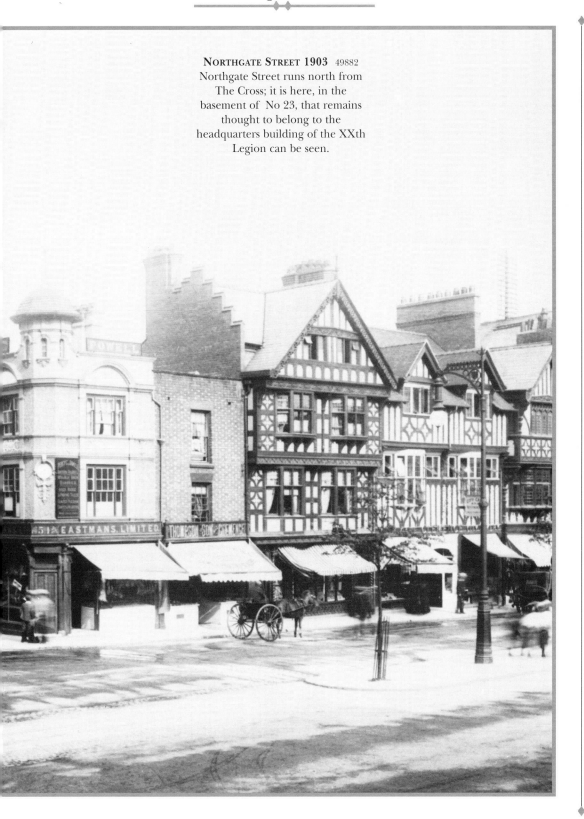

THE GUILDHALL 1888 20593
The Guildhall is to the west of the cathedral. It was designed in the Italian style and completed in 1869; the tower is 160ft high.

YE OLDE BLUE BELL, NORTHGATE STREET 1929 82757
Ye Olde Blue Bell and Ye Olde Cabin both date from the 15th century. It was off to the pub for a pint of mild, best mild or best bitter; to the cabin for ices and iced drinks in summer and hot drinks (Bovril or Oxo) in winter.

ST JOHN'S PRIORY 1913 66100
Construction of St John's Priory was begun about 1075-76 when the Bishop of Lichfield, Peter de Leia, transferred the seat of his diocese to Chester. There was an earlier Saxon church on the site; according to local legend, King Harold survived the Battle of Hastings, lived out the remainder of his life in seclusion at Chester, and was buried in St John's.

ST JOHN'S PRIORY, LOOKING WEST 1913 66099

The present church of St John's occupies the nave of the former priory; the choir and chancel were destroyed in 1470 when the central tower collapsed. The north-west tower, rebuilt around 1523, collapsed in 1573 and destroyed the west front. Following the collapse of the north-west tower, a detached belfry was erected on its site; but this too collapsed in 1881 and wrecked the north porch.

ST JOHN'S PRIORY 1888 20625

The north porch was restored in the Early English style in 1882, and a new belfry erected in 1886. When this picture was taken, visitors wishing to see round the ruins had to get the key to the gate from the sexton. If he could not be found in the church, they were advised to contact him at No 1 Lumley Place.

ST JOHN'S CHURCH 1888 20621

St John's contains several interesting features. The organ was acquired secondhand from Westminster Abbey; it had been used at the coronation of Queen Victoria. On the south wall is Diana Warburton's monument; it is unusual in that she is depicted as a skeleton holding her winding sheet upon which is written her obituary.

GROSVENOR PARK ENTRANCE 1923 73871a

On the right is St John's Church, the interior of which is considered to be one of the finest examples of Norman architecture. Though the arches and pillars date from the late 11th century, the triforium is in the transitional style of around 1200.

THE RIVER DEE AND ST MARY'S CHURCH 1906 55280

This view looks across the river to the suburb of Handbridge. The church of St Mary-without-the-Walls was completed in 1887; its distinctive spire is something of a local landmark. Nestling on its sandstone ridge in a loop in the Dee, Chester is closely framed on two sides by water. Below the weir at Old Dee Bridge the river was used for commerce, before silting-up prevented sea-going vessels reaching the city. Above the weir, the river winds around The Meadows and becomes an attractive natural playground.

GROSVENOR BRIDGE 1888 20626

When it was built in 1832, the Grosvenor Bridge was said to have the longest single stone arch span in Europe (200ft). It provided a crossing of the Dee from the Watergate to nearby Curzon Park, as well as for traffic heading to and from the direction of Wrexham.

OLD DEE BRIDGE 1923 73881

There has been a bridge over the river at this point for centuries. The old bridge with its seven irregular arches dates from the late 13th century, and was partially rebuilt in 1347-58. On the south side of the river it was once protected by a barbican - a fortified gatehouse - as a defence against Welsh raiders.

THE RIVER 1891 28891

Hugh Lupus, the first of the Norman earls of Chester, is said to have ordered the construction of a weir so that the mills would have a regular source of water power. There were mills along the banks of the Dee until 1909. On the left is the City Floating Bath, not as unusual as you might at first think: there was a floating bath at Liverpool in the early 1820s.

THE SUSPENSION BRIDGE 1888 20627

In 1852 a suspension bridge was built over the Dee to link the suburb of Queen's Park with the Groves on the north side of the river. In the distance can be seen the mills and the Old Dee Bridge. The suspension bridge was rebuilt in 1923.

THE SUSPENSION BRIDGE 1914 67546
As can be seen from this and picture No 73878,
the original suspension bridge was fairly
narrow and unable to take any wheeled vehicle
except for invalid carriages and perambulators.

QUEEN'S PARK BRIDGE 1923 73878

QUEEN'S PARK BRIDGE 1923
The rebuilt suspension bridge in 1923 shortly after its opening. Apart from the fashions of the day, this view remains virtually the same today.

◆

QUEEN'S PARK BRIDGE 1923
An excellent view of the rebuilt suspension bridge, which is for pedestrians only. On the far bank is one of the stages for excursion steamers, and a station for the hire of rowing boats.

QUEEN'S PARK BRIDGE 1923 73879

THE GROVES 1914 67544
Children fish for minnows, adults relax and enjoy the waterside scene. Behind the Edwardian bandstand is the suspension bridge across the river to Queen's Park.

THE GROVES 1923 73874
Being well-turned-out was an important part of social life in the twenties; a stroll along The Groves on a sunny summer day was an excellent opportunity to see and be seen.

THE GROVES 1888 20628

THE GROVES 1888

Since the middle of the 19th century, The Groves have provided a popular recreation area along the side of the Dee. However, the lack of people in this picture is probably due to the Frith cameraman obeying company instructions. Pictures such as this with little in the way to give their age away were taken for publication as postcards. They could be kept in print for years.

◆

THE RIVER DEE 1923

Looking across the Dee towards The Groves. The motor launches are proving a popular attraction for those wishing to take the river journey to Eaton Hall.

THE RIVER DEE 1923 73882

ST PAUL'S CHURCH AND THE RIVER DEE 1914 67547

ST PAUL'S CHURCH AND THE RIVER DEE 1914
This view was taken from The Meadows. Also prominent is the Old Chester waterworks pumping station, identified here by its tall chimney; it was demolished in 1939.

◆

THE RIVER DEE 1923
A clipper-bowed excursion steamer crowded with passengers heads along the Dee, attracting little attention from the young fishermen on the bank. Net fishing for salmon is one of the oldest industries in Chester. At one time there were sufficient salmon to support a community of netsmen, many of whom lived in Handbridge.

THE RIVER DEE 1923 73871

ECCLESTON
The Ferry c1886 1722
The three-mile trip along the Dee to Eccleston Ferry was, and remains, a popular summer season excursion. Here we have a small paddle steamer on the Eccleston Ferry/Eaton Hall run. Visitors to Eaton Hall could alight here and walk through the park to the Hall, or go on a little further to Eaton Iron Bridge.

ECCLESTON
The Ferry 1895 36455
The flat-bottomed ferry across the Dee at
Eccleston (fare 1d) was attached to both sides of
the river by cables and winched across. The ferry
would have been capable of transporting horses,
carts, waggons and coaches.

ECCLESTON, THE FERRY 1895 36454
An elderly lady is ferried across the Dee in a rowing-boat to save her having to wait for the large ferry to fill up.

ECCLESTON, THE FERRY 1903 49887a
These were the days when blazers and boaters were de rigueur for a trip down the river to Eccleston. In this picture we can see the winch mechanism and cables of the ferry; it looks as though it will be a while before a crossing is made. At this time the fare on the steamer between Chester and Eccleston was about 6d each way, and 8d each way between Chester and Eaton Iron Bridge.

ECCLESTON, THE FERRY c1965 E17004
Sixty years or so on from picture No 49887a. The ferry across the Dee has been consigned to history, and motor cruisers have replaced the sturdy well-built rowing-boats.

ECCLESTON, THE VILLAGE c1965 E17009
Many a year has passed since Mrs Gillam ran a small general shop in the village, stocking all manner of things from mops and buckets to sugar and sweets.

ECCLESTON, THE PUMP AND POST OFFICE c1955 E17002

ECCLESTON, THE CHURCH 1888 20631

This photograph shows Eccleston church about ten years before it was rebuilt in the style of the 14th century by G F Bodley; the work was paid for by the first Duke of Westminster.

SHOTWICK, THE VILLAGE c1955 S554001

EATON HALL 1914 67528
A few miles outside Chester stands Eaton Hall, the
seat of the Duke of Westminster. The present Hall,
the third on the site, was built in the grand
Victorian-Gothic style between 1869 and 1882,
designed by architect Sir Alfred Waterhouse.

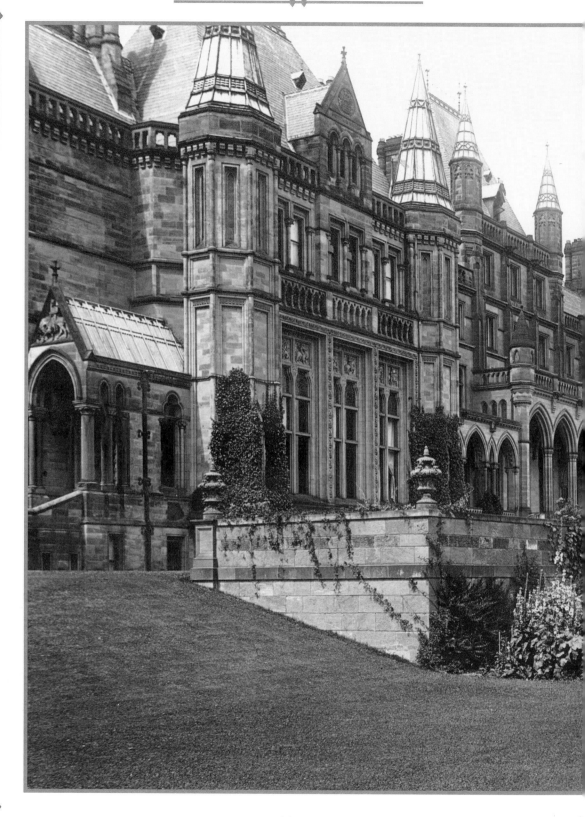

Eaton Hall 1914 67532
Visitors to the Hall could travel from Chester
not only by river steamer but also by means of
a public brake (except on Sundays) for a fare
of 1s, return 1s 6d. Admission charges were 6d
each for the Hall and gardens; tickets were
available in Chester from either the Grosvenor
Hotel or from local bookshops.

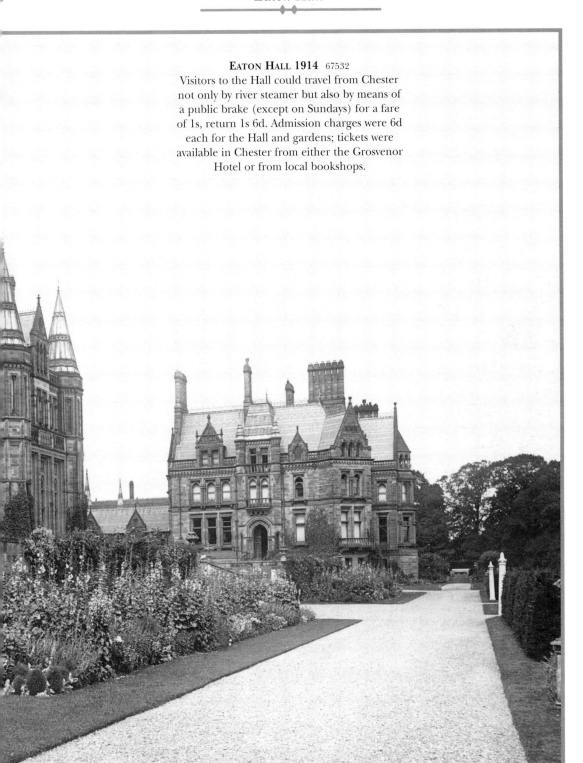

Index

Frith Book Co Titles

www.francisfrith.co.uk

The Frith Book Company publishes over 100 new titles each year. A selection of those currently available are listed below. For latest catalogue please contact Frith Book Co.

Town Books 96 pages, approx 100 photos. County and Themed Books 128 pages, approx 150 photos (unless specified). All titles hardback laminated case and jacket except those indicated pb (paperback)

Amersham, Chesham & Rickmansworth (pb)			Derby (pb)	1-85937-367-4	£9.99
	1-85937-340-2	£9.99	Derbyshire (pb)	1-85937-196-5	£9.99
Ancient Monuments & Stone Circles	1-85937-143-4	£17.99	Devon (pb)	1-85937-297-x	£9.99
Aylesbury (pb)	1-85937-227-9	£9.99	Dorset (pb)	1-85937-269-4	£9.99
Bakewell	1-85937-113-2	£12.99	Dorset Churches	1-85937-172-8	£17.99
Barnstaple (pb)	1-85937-300-3	£9.99	Dorset Coast (pb)	1-85937-299-6	£9.99
Bath (pb)	1-85937419-0	£9.99	Dorset Living Memories	1-85937-210-4	£14.99
Bedford (pb)	1-85937-205-8	£9.99	Down the Severn	1-85937-118-3	£14.99
Berkshire (pb)	1-85937-191-4	£9.99	Down the Thames (pb)	1-85937-278-3	£9.99
Berkshire Churches	1-85937-170-1	£17.99	Down the Trent	1-85937-311-9	£14.99
Blackpool (pb)	1-85937-382-8	£9.99	Dublin (pb)	1-85937-231-7	£9.99
Bognor Regis (pb)	1-85937-431-x	£9.99	East Anglia (pb)	1-85937-265-1	£9.99
Bournemouth	1-85937-067-5	£12.99	East London	1-85937-080-2	£14.99
Bradford (pb)	1-85937-204-x	£9.99	East Sussex	1-85937-130-2	£14.99
Brighton & Hove(pb)	1-85937-192-2	£8.99	Eastbourne	1-85937-061-6	£12.99
Bristol (pb)	1-85937-264-3	£9.99	Edinburgh (pb)	1-85937-193-0	£8.99
British Life A Century Ago (pb)	1-85937-213-9	£9.99	England in the 1880s	1-85937-331-3	£17.99
Buckinghamshire (pb)	1-85937-200-7	£9.99	English Castles (pb)	1-85937-434-4	£9.99
Camberley (pb)	1-85937-222-8	£9.99	English Country Houses	1-85937-161-2	£17.99
Cambridge (pb)	1-85937-422-0	£9.99	Essex (pb)	1-85937-270-8	£9.99
Cambridgeshire (pb)	1-85937-420-4	£9.99	Exeter	1-85937-126-4	£12.99
Canals & Waterways (pb)	1-85937-291-0	£9.99	Exmoor	1-85937-132-9	£14.99
Canterbury Cathedral (pb)	1-85937-179-5	£9.99	Falmouth	1-85937-066-7	£12.99
Cardiff (pb)	1-85937-093-4	£9.99	Folkestone (pb)	1-85937-124-8	£9.99
Carmarthenshire	1-85937-216-3	£14.99	Glasgow (pb)	1-85937-190-6	£9.99
Chelmsford (pb)	1-85937-310-0	£9.99	Gloucestershire	1-85937-102-7	£14.99
Cheltenham (pb)	1-85937-095-0	£9.99	Great Yarmouth (pb)	1-85937-426-3	£9.99
Cheshire (pb)	1-85937-271-6	£9.99	Greater Manchester (pb)	1-85937-266-x	£9.99
Chester	1-85937-090-x	£12.99	Guildford (pb)	1-85937-410-7	£9.99
Chesterfield	1-85937-378-x	£9.99	Hampshire (pb)	1-85937-279-1	£9.99
Chichester (pb)	1-85937-228-7	£9.99	Hampshire Churches (pb)	1-85937-207-4	£9.99
Colchester (pb)	1-85937-188-4	£8.99	Harrogate	1-85937-423-9	£9.99
Cornish Coast	1-85937-163-9	£14.99	Hastings & Bexhill (pb)	1-85937-131-0	£9.99
Cornwall (pb)	1-85937-229-5	£9.99	Heart of Lancashire (pb)	1-85937-197-3	£9.99
Cornwall Living Memories	1-85937-248-1	£14.99	Helston (pb)	1-85937-214-7	£9.99
Cotswolds (pb)	1-85937-230-9	£9.99	Hereford (pb)	1-85937-175-2	£9.99
Cotswolds Living Memories	1-85937-255-4	£14.99	Herefordshire	1-85937-174-4	£14.99
County Durham	1-85937-123-x	£14.99	Hertfordshire (pb)	1-85937-247-3	£9.99
Croydon Living Memories	1-85937-162-0	£9.99	Horsham (pb)	1-85937-432-8	£9.99
Cumbria	1-85937-101-9	£14.99	Humberside	1-85937-215-5	£14.99
Dartmoor	1-85937-145-0	£14.99	Hythe, Romney Marsh & Ashford	1-85937-256-2	£9.99

Available from your local bookshop or from the publisher

Frith Book Co Titles (continued)

Title	ISBN	Price	Title	ISBN	Price
Ipswich (pb)	1-85937-424-7	£9.99	St Ives (pb)	1-85937415-8	£9.99
Ireland (pb)	1-85937-181-7	£9.99	Scotland (pb)	1-85937-182-5	£9.99
Isle of Man (pb)	1-85937-268-6	£9.99	Scottish Castles (pb)	1-85937-323-2	£9.99
Isles of Scilly	1-85937-136-1	£14.99	Sevenoaks & Tunbridge	1-85937-057-8	£12.99
Isle of Wight (pb)	1-85937-429-8	£9.99	Sheffield, South Yorks (pb)	1-85937-267-8	£9.99
Isle of Wight Living Memories	1-85937-304-6	£14.99	Shrewsbury (pb)	1-85937-325-9	£9.99
Kent (pb)	1-85937-189-2	£9.99	Shropshire (pb)	1-85937-326-7	£9.99
Kent Living Memories	1-85937-125-6	£14.99	Somerset	1-85937-153-1	£14.99
Lake District (pb)	1-85937-275-9	£9.99	South Devon Coast	1-85937-107-8	£14.99
Lancaster, Morecambe & Heysham (pb)	1-85937-233-3	£9.99	South Devon Living Memories	1-85937-168-x	£14.99
Leeds (pb)	1-85937-202-3	£9.99	South Hams	1-85937-220-1	£14.99
Leicester	1-85937-073-x	£12.99	Southampton (pb)	1-85937-427-1	£9.99
Leicestershire (pb)	1-85937-185-x	£9.99	Southport (pb)	1-85937-425-5	£9.99
Lincolnshire (pb)	1-85937-433-6	£9.99	Staffordshire	1-85937-047-0	£12.99
Liverpool & Merseyside (pb)	1-85937-234-1	£9.99	Stratford upon Avon	1-85937-098-5	£12.99
London (pb)	1-85937-183-3	£9.99	Suffolk (pb)	1-85937-221-x	£9.99
Ludlow (pb)	1-85937-176-0	£9.99	Suffolk Coast	1-85937-259-7	£14.99
Luton (pb)	1-85937-235-x	£9.99	Surrey (pb)	1-85937-240-6	£9.99
Maidstone	1-85937-056-x	£14.99	Sussex (pb)	1-85937-184-1	£9.99
Manchester (pb)	1-85937-198-1	£9.99	Swansea (pb)	1-85937-167-1	£9.99
Middlesex	1-85937-158-2	£14.99	Tees Valley & Cleveland	1-85937-211-2	£14.99
New Forest	1-85937-128-0	£14.99	Thanet (pb)	1-85937-116-7	£9.99
Newark (pb)	1-85937-366-6	£9.99	Tiverton (pb)	1-85937-178-7	£9.99
Newport, Wales (pb)	1-85937-258-9	£9.99	Torbay	1-85937-063-2	£12.99
Newquay (pb)	1-85937-421-2	£9.99	Truro	1-85937-147-7	£12.99
Norfolk (pb)	1-85937-195-7	£9.99	Victorian and Edwardian Cornwall	1-85937-252-x	£14.99
Norfolk Living Memories	1-85937-217-1	£14.99	Victorian & Edwardian Devon	1-85937-253-8	£14.99
Northamptonshire	1-85937-150-7	£14.99	Victorian & Edwardian Kent	1-85937-149-3	£14.99
Northumberland Tyne & Wear (pb)	1-85937-281-3	£9.99	Vic & Ed Maritime Album	1-85937-144-2	£17.99
North Devon Coast	1-85937-146-9	£14.99	Victorian and Edwardian Sussex	1-85937-157-4	£14.99
North Devon Living Memories	1-85937-261-9	£14.99	Victorian & Edwardian Yorkshire	1-85937-154-x	£14.99
North London	1-85937-206-6	£14.99	Victorian Seaside	1-85937-159-0	£17.99
North Wales (pb)	1-85937-298-8	£9.99	Villages of Devon (pb)	1-85937-293-7	£9.99
North Yorkshire (pb)	1-85937-236-8	£9.99	Villages of Kent (pb)	1-85937-294-5	£9.99
Norwich (pb)	1-85937-194-9	£8.99	Villages of Sussex (pb)	1-85937-295-3	£9.99
Nottingham (pb)	1-85937-324-0	£9.99	Warwickshire (pb)	1-85937-203-1	£9.99
Nottinghamshire (pb)	1-85937-187-6	£9.99	Welsh Castles (pb)	1-85937-322-4	£9.99
Oxford (pb)	1-85937-411-5	£9.99	West Midlands (pb)	1-85937-289-9	£9.99
Oxfordshire (pb)	1-85937-430-1	£9.99	West Sussex	1-85937-148-5	£14.99
Peak District (pb)	1-85937-280-5	£9.99	West Yorkshire (pb)	1-85937-201-5	£9.99
Penzance	1-85937-069-1	£12.99	Weymouth (pb)	1-85937-209-0	£9.99
Peterborough (pb)	1-85937-219-8	£9.99	Wiltshire (pb)	1-85937-277-5	£9.99
Piers	1-85937-237-6	£17.99	Wiltshire Churches (pb)	1-85937-171-x	£9.99
Plymouth	1-85937-119-1	£12.99	Wiltshire Living Memories	1-85937-245-7	£14.99
Poole & Sandbanks (pb)	1-85937-251-1	£9.99	Winchester (pb)	1-85937-428-x	£9.99
Preston (pb)	1-85937-212-0	£9.99	Windmills & Watermills	1-85937-242-2	£17.99
Reading (pb)	1-85937-238-4	£9.99	Worcester (pb)	1-85937-165-5	£9.99
Romford (pb)	1-85937-319-4	£9.99	Worcestershire	1-85937-152-3	£14.99
Salisbury (pb)	1-85937-239-2	£9.99	York (pb)	1-85937-199-x	£9.99
Scarborough (pb)	1-85937-379-8	£9.99	Yorkshire (pb)	1-85937-186-8	£9.99
St Albans (pb)	1-85937-341-0	£9.99	Yorkshire Living Memories	1-85937-166-3	£14.99

See Frith books on the internet www.francisfrith.co.uk

FRITH PRODUCTS & SERVICES

Francis Frith would doubtless be pleased to know that the pioneering publishing venture he started in 1860 still continues today. A hundred and forty years later, The Francis Frith Collection continues in the same innovative tradition and is now one of the foremost publishers of vintage photographs in the world. Some of the current activities include:

Interior Decoration

Today Frith's photographs can be seen framed and as giant wall murals in thousands of pubs, restaurants, hotels, banks, retail stores and other public buildings throughout the country. In every case they enhance the unique local atmosphere of the places they depict and provide reminders of gentler days in an increasingly busy and frenetic world.

Product Promotions

Frith products are used by many major companies to promote the sales of their own products or to reinforce their own history and heritage. Frith promotions have been used by Hovis bread, Courage beers, Scots Porage Oats, Colman's mustard, Cadbury's foods, Mellow Birds coffee, Dunhill pipe tobacco, Guinness, and Bulmer's Cider.

Genealogy and Family History

As the interest in family history and roots grows world-wide, more and more people are turning to Frith's photographs of Great Britain for images of the towns, villages and streets where their ancestors lived; and, of course, photographs of the churches and chapels where their ancestors were christened, married and buried are an essential part of every genealogy tree and family album.

Frith Products

All Frith photographs are available Framed or just as Mounted Prints and Posters (size 23 x 16 inches). These may be ordered from the address below. From time to time other products - Address Books, Calendars, Table Mats, etc - are available.

The Internet

Already twenty thousand Frith photographs can be viewed and purchased on the internet through the Frith websites and a myriad of partner sites.

For more detailed information on Frith companies and products, look at these sites:

> www.francisfrith.co.uk
> www.francisfrith.com
> *(for North American visitors)*

See the complete list of Frith Books at:

www.francisfrith.co.uk

This web site is regularly updated with the latest list of publications from the Frith Book Company. If you wish to buy books relating to another part of the country that your local bookshop does not stock, you may purchase on-line.

For further information, trade, or author enquiries please contact us at the address below:
The Francis Frith Collection, Frith's Barn, Teffont, Salisbury, Wiltshire, England SP3 5QP.
Tel: +44 (0)1722 716 376 Fax: +44 (0)1722 716 881 Email: sales@francisfrith.co.uk

See Frith books on the internet www.francisfrith.co.uk

TO RECEIVE YOUR FREE MOUNTED PRINT

Mounted Print
Overall size 14 x 11 inches

Cut out this Voucher and return it with your remittance for £1.95 to cover postage and handling, to UK addresses. For overseas addresses please include £4.00 post and handling. Choose any photograph included in this book. Your SEPIA print will be A4 in size, and mounted in a cream mount with burgundy rule line, overall size 14 x 11 inches.

Order additional Mounted Prints at HALF PRICE (only £7.49 each*)

If there are further pictures you would like to order, possibly as gifts for friends and family, purchase them at half price (no additional postage and handling required).

Have your Mounted Prints framed*

For an additional £14.95 per print you can have your chosen Mounted Print framed in an elegant polished wood and gilt moulding, overall size 16 x 13 inches (no additional postage and handling required).

---

* IMPORTANT!
These special prices are only available if ordered using the original voucher on this page (no copies permitted) and at the same time as your free Mounted Print, for delivery to the same address

---

Frith Collectors' Guild

From time to time we publish a magazine of news and stories about Frith photographs and further special offers of Frith products. If you would like 12 months FREE membership, please return this form.

Send completed forms to:

The Francis Frith Collection, Frith's Barn, Teffont, Salisbury, Wiltshire SP3 5QP

$\mathcal{V}$oucher for FREE and Reduced Price Frith Prints

Picture no.	Page number	Qty	Mounted @ £7.49	Framed + £14.95	Total Cost
		1	**Free of charge***	£	£
			£7.49	£	£
			£7.49	£	£
			£7.49	£	£
			£7.49	£	£
			£7.49	£	£

Please allow 28 days for delivery	*** Post & handling**	**£1.95**
Book Title	**Total Order Cost**	**£**

Please do not photocopy this voucher. Only the original is valid, so please cut it out and return it to us.

I enclose a cheque / postal order for £ . . . .
made payable to 'The Francis Frith Collection'
OR please debit my Mastercard / Visa / Switch / Amex card
(credit cards please on all overseas orders)

Number . . . .

Issue No(Switch only) . . . . .Valid from (Amex/Switch) . . . .

Expires . . . . Signature . . . .

Name Mr/Mrs/Ms . . . .

Address . . . .

. . . .

. . . . Postcode . . . .

Daytime Tel No . . . .   Valid to 31/12/02

The Francis Frith Collectors' Guild

Please enrol me as a member for 12 months free of charge.

Name Mr/Mrs/Ms . . . .

Address . . . .

. . . .

. . . . Postcode . . . .

Would you like to find out more about Francis Frith?

We have recently recruited some entertaining speakers who are happy to visit local groups, clubs and societies to give an illustrated talk documenting Frith's travels and photographs. If you are a member of such a group and are interested in hosting a presentation, we would love to hear from you.

Our speakers bring with them a small selection of our local town and county books, together with sample prints. They are happy to take orders. A small proportion of the order value is donated to the group who have hosted the presentation. The talks are therefore an excellent way of fundraising for small groups and societies.

Can you help us with information about any of the Frith photographs in this book?

We are gradually compiling an historical record for each of the photographs in the Frith archive. It is always fascinating to find out the names of the people shown in the pictures, as well as insights into the shops, buildings and other features depicted.

If you recognize anyone in the photographs in this book, or if you have information not already included in the author's caption, do let us know. We would love to hear from you, and will try to publish it in future books or articles.

Our production team

Frith books are produced by a small dedicated team at offices in the converted Grade II listed 18th-century barn at Teffont near Salisbury, illustrated above. Most have worked with the Frith Collection for many years. All have in common one quality: they have a passion for the Frith Collection. The team is constantly expanding, but currently includes:

Jason Buck, John Buck, Douglas Burns, Heather Crisp, Isobel Hall, Rob Hames, Hazel Heaton, Peter Horne, James Kinnear, Tina Leary, Hannah Marsh, Eliza Sackett, Terence Sackett, Sandra Sanger, Shelley Tolcher, Susanna Walker, Clive Wathen and Jenny Wathen.

Free Print - see overleaf